Jan. 05

Ginger,
We pray Gods continued
strength & wisdom as you
apply this principles to your
Life!

In His Awesome
Love,
Pastor Larry & Michelle

EQUIPPING

101

EQUIPPING

101

WHAT EVERY LEADER NEEDS TO KNOW

JOHN C. MAXWELL

THOMAS NELSON PUBLISHERS®
Nashville

A Division of Thomas Nelson, Inc.
www.ThomasNelson.com

Published in Nashville, Tennessee, by Thomas Nelson, Inc.

Portions of this book have been taken from *Developing the Leaders
Around You, The 17 Essential Qualities of a Team Player,* and
The 17 Indisputable Laws of Teamwork.

Library of Congress Cataloging-in-Publication Data

Maxwell, John C., 1947–
Equipping 101 / John C. Maxwell.
p. cm.
Includes bibliographical references.
ISBN 0-7852-6352-7 (hardcover)
1. Teams in the workplace. 2. Leadership. 3. Career development.
4. Mentoring. I. Title.
HD66.M377 2004
658.3'14—dc22
2003021379

Printed in the United States of America

03 04 05 06 07 PHX 5 4 3 2 1

CONTENTS

Publisher's Preface

Look at the most successful organizations in the world, and you find not just one leader—you'll see many strong leaders working together to create their success. That doesn't happen by accident. The most successful organizations possess leaders who are equipping others around them, whether that organization is a small business, large corporation, nonprofit, or sports team. When a leader is dedicated to the equipping process, the level of performance within the whole organization rises dramatically.

Fred A. Manske Jr. said, "The greatest leader is willing to train people and develop them to the point that they eventually surpass him or her in knowledge and ability." This volume, by Dr. John C. Maxwell, will help you to unlock the hidden abilities in your people by teaching you to equip them for excellence. "Success for leaders," says Maxwell, "can be defined as the maximum utilization of the abilities of those around them." Maxwell should know. He is someone who has made equipping and developing others the primary focus of his life for over twenty years.

In this concise book, a companion to *Relationships 101, Attitude 101,* and *Leadership 101,* you will be equipped yourself: Not only will you learn why equipping others to lead is the most powerful method for success, but you will also learn how to identify potential leaders, equip them, and then take them to a whole new level once they've been released to lead. It's a process that creates synergy in your organization for the long haul.

PART 1

EQUIPPING FOR SUCCESS

WHY DO I NEED TO EQUIP OTHERS?

One is too small a number to achieve greatness.

Who are your personal heroes? Okay, maybe you don't have heroes exactly. Then let me ask you this: Which people do you admire most? Who do you wish you were more like? What people fire you up and get your juices flowing? Do you admire . . .

- Business innovators, such as Sam Walton, Fred Smith, or Bill Gates?

- Great athletes, such as Michael Jordan, Tiger Woods, or Mark McGwire?

- Creative geniuses, such as Pablo Picasso, Buckminster Fuller, or Wolfgang Amadeus Mozart?

- Pop culture icons, such as Marilyn Monroe, Andy Warhol, or Elvis Presley?

- Spiritual leaders, such as John Wesley, Billy Graham, or Mother Teresa?

- Political leaders, such as Alexander the Great, Charlemagne, or Winston Churchill?

- Film industry giants, such as D. W. Griffith, Charlie Chaplin, or Steven Spielberg?

- Architects and engineers, such as Frank Lloyd Wright, the Starrett brothers, or Joseph Strauss?

- Revolutionary thinkers, such as Marie Curie, Thomas Edison, or Albert Einstein?

Or maybe your list includes people in a field I didn't mention.

It's safe to say that we all admire achievers. And we Americans especially love pioneers and bold individualists, people who fight alone, despite the odds or opposition: the settler who carves a place for himself in the wilds of the frontier, the Old West sheriff who resolutely faces an enemy in a gunfight, the pilot who bravely flies solo across the Atlantic Ocean, and the scientist who changes the world through the power of his mind.

THE MYTH OF THE LONE RANGER

As much as we admire solo achievement, the truth is that no lone individual has done anything of value. The belief that one person can do something great is a myth. There are no real Rambos who can take on a hostile army by themselves. Even the Lone Ranger wasn't really a loner. Everywhere he went he rode with Tonto!

Nothing of significance was ever achieved by an individual acting alone. Look below the surface and you will find that all seemingly solo acts are really team efforts. Frontiersman Daniel Boone had companions from the Transylvania Company as he blazed the Wilderness Road. Sheriff Wyatt Earp had his two brothers and Doc Holliday looking out for him. Aviator Charles Lindbergh had the backing of nine businessmen from St. Louis and the services of the Ryan Aeronautical Company, which built his plane. Even Albert Einstein, the scientist who revolutionized the world with his theory of relativity, didn't work in a vacuum. Of the debt he owed to others for his work, Einstein once remarked, "Many times a day I realize how much my own outer and inner life is built upon the labors of my fellow men, both living and dead, and how earnestly I must exert myself in order to give in return as much as I have received." It's true that the history of our country is marked by the accomplishments of many strong leaders and innovative individuals who took considerable risks. But those people always were part of teams.

Economist Lester C. Thurow commented on the subject:

> There is nothing antithetical in American history, culture, or traditions to teamwork. Teams were important in America's history—wagon trains conquered the West, men working together on the assembly line in American industry conquered the world, a successful national strategy and a lot of teamwork put an American on the moon first (and thus far, last). But American mythology extols only the individual . . . In America, halls of fame exist for almost every conceivable activity, but nowhere do Americans raise monuments in praise of teamwork.

I must say that I don't agree with all of Thurow's conclusions. After all, I've seen the U.S. Marine Corps war memorial in Washington, D.C., commemorating the raising of the flag on Iwo Jima. But he is right about something. Teamwork is and always has been essential to building this country. And that statement can be made about every country around the world.

A Chinese proverb states, "Behind an able man there are always other able men." And the truth is that teamwork is at the heart of great achievement. The question isn't whether teams have value. The question is whether we acknowledge that fact and become better team players. That's why I assert that one is too small a number to achieve greatness. You cannot do anything of real value alone. If you truly take this to heart, you will begin to see the value of developing and equipping your team players.

"BEHIND AN ABLE MAN THERE ARE ALWAYS
OTHER ABLE MEN."—CHINESE PROVERB

I challenge you to think of one act of genuine significance in the history of humankind that was performed by a lone human being. No matter what you name, you will find that a team of people was involved. That is why President Lyndon Johnson said, "There are no problems we cannot solve together, and very few that we can solve by ourselves."

C. Gene Wilkes, in his book, *Jesus on Leadership,* observed that the power of teams not only is evident in today's modern business world, but it also has a deep history that is evident even in biblical times. Wilkes asserts:

- Teams involve more people, thus affording more resources, ideas, and energy than would an individual.

- Teams maximize a leader's potential and minimize her weaknesses. Strengths and weaknesses are more exposed in individuals.

- Teams provide multiple perspectives on how to meet a need or reach a goal, thus devising several alternatives for each situation.

- Teams share the credit for victories and the blame for losses. This fosters genuine humility and authentic community.

- Teams keep leaders accountable for the goal.

- Teams can simply do more than an individual.

If you want to reach your potential or strive for the seemingly impossible—such as communicating your message two thousand years after you are gone—you need to become a team player. It may be a cliché, but it is nonetheless true: Individuals play the game, but teams win championships.

WHY DO WE STAND ALONE?

Knowing all that we do about the potential of teams, why do some people still want to do things by themselves? I believe there are a number of reasons.

1. EGO

Few people are fond of admitting that they can't do everything, yet that is a reality of life. There are no supermen or superwomen. So the question is not whether you can do everything by yourself; it's how soon you're going to realize that you can't.

Philanthropist Andrew Carnegie declared, "It marks a big step in your development when you come to realize that other people can help you do a better job than you could do alone." To do something really big, let go of your ego, and get ready to be part of a team.

2. Insecurity

In my work with leaders, I've found that some individuals fail to promote teamwork and fail to equip their team members for leadership because they feel threatened by other people. Sixteenth-century Florentine statesman Niccolò Machiavelli probably made similar observations, prompting him to write, "The first method for estimating the intelligence of a ruler is to look at the men he has around him."

I believe that insecurity, rather than poor judgment or lack of intelligence, most often causes leaders to surround themselves with weak people. Only secure leaders give power to others. On the other hand, insecure leaders usually fail to build teams because of one of two reasons: Either they want to maintain control over everything for which they are responsible, or they fear being replaced by someone more capable. In either case, leaders who fail to promote teamwork undermine their own potential and erode the best efforts of the people with whom they work. They would benefit from the advice of President Woodrow Wilson: "We should not only use all the brains we have, but all that we can borrow."

"THE FIRST METHOD FOR ESTIMATING THE INTELLIGENCE OF A RULER IS TO LOOK AT THE MEN HE HAS AROUND HIM."—NICCOLÒ MACHIAVELLI

---

3. NAIVETÉ

Consultant John Ghegan keeps a sign on his desk that says, "If I had it to do all over again, I'd get help." That remark accurately represents the feelings of the third type of people who fail to become team builders. They naively underestimate the difficulty of achieving big things. As a result, they try to go it alone.

Some people who start out in this group turn out okay in the end. They discover that their dreams are bigger than their capabilities, they realize they won't accomplish their goals solo, and they adjust. They make team building their approach to achievement. But some others learn the truth too late, and as a result, they never accomplish their goals. And that's a shame.

4. TEMPERAMENT

Some people aren't very outgoing and simply don't think in terms of team building and equipping. As they face challenges, it never occurs to them to enlist others to achieve something.

As a people person, I find that hard to relate to. Whenever I face any kind of challenge, the very first thing I do is to think about the people I want on the team to help with it. I've been that way since I was a kid. I've always thought, *Why take the journey alone when you can invite others along with you?*

I understand that not everyone operates that way. But whether or not you are naturally inclined to be part of a team is really irrelevant. If you do everything alone and never partner with other people, you create huge barriers to your own potential. Dr. Allan Fromme quipped, "People have been known to achieve more as a result of working with others than against them." What an understatement! It takes a team to do anything of lasting value. Besides, even the most introverted person in the world can learn to enjoy the benefits of being on a team. (That's true even if someone isn't trying to accomplish something great.)

A few years ago my friend Chuck Swindoll wrote a piece in *The Finishing Touch* that sums up the importance of teamwork. He said,

Nobody is a whole team . . . We need each other. You need someone and someone needs you. Isolated islands we're not. To make this thing called life work, we gotta lean and support. And relate and respond. And give and take. And confess and forgive. And reach out and embrace and rely . . . Since none of us is a whole, independent, self-sufficient, super-capable, all-powerful hotshot, let's quit acting like we are. Life's lonely enough without our playing that silly role. The game is over. Let's link up.

For the person trying to do everything alone, the game really is over. If you want to do something big, you must link up with others. One is too small a number to achieve greatness.

How Can I Adopt
a Team Mind-Set?

Investing in a team almost guarantees a high return for the effort, because a team can do so much more than individuals.

He's one of the greatest team builders in all of sports, yet you've probably never heard of him. Here is a list of his impressive accomplishments:

- Forty consecutive basketball seasons with at least twenty wins

- Five national championships

- Number one ranking in his region in twenty of the last thirty-three years

- Lifetime winning percentage of .870

His name is Morgan Wootten. And why have most people never heard of him? Because he is a high school basketball coach!

When asked to name the greatest basketball coach of all time, most people would respond with one of two names: Red Auerbach or John Wooden. But do you know what John Wooden, the UCLA coach called the Wizard of Westwood, had to say about Morgan Wootten? He was emphatic in his appraisal: "People say Morgan Wootten is the best high school coach in the country. I disagree. I know of no finer coach at any level—high school, college or pro. I've said it elsewhere and I'll say it here: I stand in awe of him."[1]

That's a pretty strong recommendation from the man who won ten NCAA national championships and coached some of the most talented players in the game, including Kareem Abdul-Jabbar. (By the way, when Kareem was in high school at Power Memorial Academy, his team lost only one game— to Morgan Wootten's team!)

No Plan to Be a Team Builder

Morgan Wootten never planned to coach a team. He was a decent athlete in high school, but nothing special. However, he was an excellent talker. When he was growing up, his ambition was to be an attorney. But when he was a nineteen-year-old college student, a friend tricked him into accepting a job coaching baseball, a game he knew little about, to kids from an orphanage. The team had no uniforms and no equipment. And despite working hard, the boys lost all sixteen of their games.

During that first season, Wootten fell in love with those kids. When they asked him to come back and coach football, he couldn't refuse them. Besides, he had played football in high school, so he knew something about it. The orphanage team went undefeated and won the Washington, D.C., Catholic Youth Organization (CYO) championship. But more important, Wootten began to realize that he wanted to invest his time in children, not in court cases.

Even that first year he made a difference in the lives of kids. He remembers one boy in particular who had started stealing and kept being brought back to the orphanage by the police. He described the boy as having "two and a half strikes against him already." Wootten let the boy know he was headed for trouble. But he also took the boy under his wing. Wootten recalled,

We started spending some time together. I took him to my house and he'd enjoy Mom's meals. He spent weekends with us. He became friends with my brother and sisters. He's still in Washington today and doing quite well and known to a lot of people. Anyone would be proud to call him their son. He was bound for a life of crime and jail, however, and maybe a lot worse, until someone gave him the greatest gift a parent can give a child—his time.

Giving of himself to the people on his teams is something Wootten has done every year since then. NCAA basketball coach Marty Fletcher, a former player and assistant under Wootten, summarized his talent this way: "His secret is that he makes whomever he is with feel like the most important person in the world."[2]

CREATING A DYNASTY

It wasn't long before Wootten was invited to become an assistant coach at a local powerhouse high school. Then with a couple of years' experience under his belt, he became head coach at DeMatha High School.

When he started at the school in 1956, Wootten was taking over a bunch of losing teams. He called together all of the students who wanted to play sports at DeMatha, and he told them:

Fellas, things are going to change. I know how bad DeMatha's teams have been during these last few years, but that's over with. We're going to win at DeMatha and we're going to build a tradition of winning. Starting right now . . . But let me tell you how we're going to do it. We're going to outwork every team we ever play . . . With a lot of hard work and discipline and dedication, people are going to hear about us and respect us, because DeMatha will be a winner.[3]

That year, the football team won half of its games, which was quite an accomplishment. In basketball and baseball, they were division champions. His teams have been winning ever since. DeMatha has long been considered a dynasty.

On October 13, 2000, Wootten was inducted into the Naismith Basketball Hall of Fame in Springfield, Massachusetts. At that time, his teams had amassed a record of 1,210-183. Over the years, more than 250 of his players have won college scholarships. Twelve players from his high school teams went on to play in the NBA.[4]

It's Not About Basketball

But winning games and honors isn't what excites Wootten most. It's investing in the kids. Wootten says,

Coaches at every level have a tendency to lose sight of their purpose at times, especially after success arrives. They

start to put the cart before the horse by working harder
and harder to develop their teams, using their boys or girls
to do it, gradually forgetting that their real purpose should
be to develop the kids, using their teams to do it.[5]

Wootten's attitude reaps rewards not only for the team, but
also for the individuals on the team. For example, for a
twenty-six-year stretch, every single one of Wootten's seniors
earned college scholarships—not just starters but bench players too.

Equipping your team compounds over time. Morgan
Wootten equips his players because it is the right thing to
do, because he cares about them. That practice has made
his players good, his teams successful, and his career
remarkable. He is the first basketball coach to have won
1,200 games at any level. Developing people pays off in
every way.

HOW TO INVEST IN YOUR TEAM

I believe that most people recognize that investing in a team
brings benefits to everyone on the team. The question for
most people isn't why, but how. Allow me to share with you
ten steps you can take to invest in your team.

Here is how to get started:

1. Make the Decision to Build a Team—This Starts the Investment in the Team

It's said that every journey begins with the first step. Deciding that people on the team are worth equipping and developing is the first step in building a better team. That requires commitment.

2. Gather the Best Team Possible—This Elevates the Potential of the Team

The better the people on the team, the greater the potential. There's only one kind of team that you may be a part of where you shouldn't go out and find the best players available, and that's family. You need to stick with those teammates through thick and thin. But every other kind of team can benefit from the recruitment of the very best people available.

3. Pay the Price to Develop the Team—This Ensures the Growth of the Team

When Morgan Wootten extended himself to benefit the kid who had two-and-a-half strikes against him, he and his family had to pay a price to help that boy. It wasn't convenient or comfortable. It cost them in energy, money, and time.

It will cost you to develop your team. You will have to dedicate time that could be used for personal productivity. You will have to spend money that could be used for personal benefit. And sometimes you will have to set aside your personal agenda.

4. DO THINGS TOGETHER AS A TEAM—THIS PROVIDES COMMUNITY FOR THE TEAM

I once read the statement, "Even when you've played the game of your life, it's the feeling of teamwork that you'll remember. You'll forget the plays, the shots, and the scores, but you'll never forget your teammates." That is describing the community that develops among teammates who spend time doing things together.

DECIDING THAT PEOPLE ON THE TEAM ARE WORTH EQUIPPING AND DEVELOPING IS THE FIRST STEP IN BUILDING A BETTER TEAM.

The only way to develop community and cohesiveness among your teammates is to get them together, not just in a professional setting but in personal ones as well. There are lots of ways to get yourself connected with your teammates, and to connect them with one another. Many families who want to bond find that camping does the trick. Business colleagues can socialize outside work (in an appropriate way). The where and when are not as important as the fact that team members share common experiences.

5. Empower Team Members with Responsibility and Authority—This Raises Up Leaders for the Team

The greatest growth for people often occurs as a result of the trial and error of personal experience. Any team that wants people to step up to a higher level of performance— and to higher levels of leadership—must give team members authority as well as responsibility. If you are a leader on your team, don't protect your position or hoard your power. Give it away. That's the only way to empower your team.

6. Give Credit for Success to the Team—This Lifts the Morale of the Team

Mark Twain said, "I can live for two months on one good compliment." That's the way most people feel. They are willing to work hard if they receive recognition for their efforts. Compliment your teammates. Talk up their accomplishments. And if you're the leader, take the blame but never the credit. Do that and your team will always fight for you.

"I can live for two months on one good compliment."—Mark Twain

---

7. Watch to See That the Investment in the Team Is Paying Off—This Brings Accountability to the Team

If you put money into an investment, you expect a return—maybe not right away, but certainly over time. How will you know whether you are gaining or losing ground on that investment? You have to pay attention to it and measure its progress.

The same is true of an investment in people. You need to observe whether you are getting a return for the time, energy, and resources you are putting into them. Some people develop quickly. Others are slower to respond, and that's okay. The main outcome you want to see is progress.

8. Stop Your Investment in Players Who Do Not Grow—This Eliminates Greater Losses for the Team

One of the most difficult experiences for any team member is leaving a teammate behind. Yet that is what you must do if someone on your team refuses to grow or change for the benefit of teammates. That doesn't mean that you love the person less. It just means you stop spending your time trying to invest in someone who won't or can't make the team better.

9. Create New Opportunities for the Team—This Allows the Team to Stretch

There is no greater investment you can make in a team than giving it new opportunities. When a team has the possibility of taking new ground or facing new challenges, it has to stretch to meet them. That process not only gives the team a chance to grow, but it also benefits every individual. Everyone has the opportunity to grow toward his or her potential.

10. Give the Team the Best Possible Chance to Succeed—This Guarantees the Team a High Return

James E. Hunton says, "Coming together is a beginning. Keeping together is progress. Working together is success." One of the most essential tasks you can undertake is to clear obstacles so that the team has the best possible chance to work toward success. If you are a team member, that may mean making a personal sacrifice or helping others to work together better. If you are a leader, that means creating an energized environment for the team and equipping each person with what he needs at any given time to ensure success.

Investing in a team almost guarantees a high return for the effort, because a team can do so much more than individuals. Or as Rex Murphy, one of my conference attendees, told me: "Where there's a will there's a way; where there's a team, there's more than one way."

My Personal Investment—and Return

Once you have experienced what it means to invest in your team, you will never be able to stop. Thinking about my team—about how the teammates add value to me as I add value to them—brings me abundant joy. And just like my investment and their return, my joy continues to compound.

At this stage of my life, everything I do is a team effort. When I first started teaching seminars, I did everything. Certainly there were other people pitching in, but I was just as likely to pack and ship a box as I was to speak. Now, I show up and teach. My wonderful team takes care of everything else. Even the book you're reading was a team effort. I would do anything for the people on my team because they do everything for me:

> My team makes me better than I am.
> My team multiplies my value to others.
> My team enables me to do what I do best.
> My team gives me more time.
> My team represents me where I cannot go.
> My team provides community for our enjoyment.
> My team fulfills the desires of my heart.

If your current team experiences are not as positive as you would like, then it's time to increase your level of investment. Building and equipping a team for the future is just like developing a financial nest egg. It may start slowly, but what you put in brings a high return—similar to the way that compound interest works with finances. Try it and you will find that investing in the team compounds over time.

PART II

EQUIPPING THE RIGHT PEOPLE

3

WHOM SHOULD
I EQUIP?

*Those closest to the leader will determine the
success level of that leader.*

One night, after working quite late, I grabbed a copy of *Sports Illustrated*, hoping its pages would lull me to sleep. It had the opposite effect. On the back cover was an advertisement that caught my eye and got my emotional juices flowing. It featured a picture of John Wooden, the coach who led the UCLA Bruins for many years. The caption beneath his picture read, "The guy who puts the ball through the hoop has ten hands."

John Wooden was a great basketball coach. Called the Wizard of Westwood, he brought ten national basketball championships to UCLA in a span of twelve years. Two back-to-back championships are almost unheard of in the world of competitive sports, but he led the Bruins to *seven titles in a row*. It took a consistent level of superior play, good coaching, and hard practice. But the key to the Bruins's success was

Coach Wooden's unyielding dedication to his concept of teamwork.

He knew that if you oversee people and you wish to develop leaders, you are responsible to: (1) appreciate them for who they are; (2) believe that they will do their very best; (3) praise their accomplishments; and (4) accept your personal responsibility to them as their leader.

Coach Bear Bryant expressed this same sentiment when he said: "I'm just a plowhand from Arkansas, but I have learned how to hold a team together—how to lift some men up, how to calm others down, until finally they've got one heartbeat together as a team. There's always just three things I say: 'If anything goes bad, I did it. If anything goes semi-good, then we did it. If anything goes real good, they did it.' That's all it takes to get people to win." Bear Bryant won people and games. Until a few years ago, he held the title of the winningest coach in the history of college football, with 323 victories.

Great leaders—the truly successful ones who are in the top 1 percent—all have one thing in common. They know that acquiring and keeping good people is a leader's most important task. An organization cannot increase its productivity—but people can! The asset that truly appreciates within any organization is people. Systems become dated. Buildings deteriorate. Machinery wears. But people can grow, develop, and become more effective if they have a leader who understands their potential value.

If you really want to be a successful leader, you must develop and equip other leaders around you. You must find a way to get your vision seen, implemented, and contributed to by your team. The leader sees the big picture, but he needs other leaders to help make his mental picture a reality.

Most leaders have followers around them. They believe the key to leadership is gaining more *followers.* Few leaders surround themselves with other *leaders,* but the ones who do bring great value to their organizations. And not only is their burden lightened, but their vision is carried on and enlarged.

Whom You Equip Really Matters

The key to surrounding yourself with other leaders is to find the best people you can, then equip them to become the best leaders they can be. Great leaders produce other leaders. Let me tell you why:

Those Closest to the Leader Will Determine the Success Level of That Leader

The greatest leadership principle that I have learned in over thirty years of leadership is that those closest to the leader will determine the success level of that leader. A negative reading of this statement is also true: Those closest to the leader will determine the level of failure for that leader. In other words, the people close to me "make me or break me." The determination of a positive or negative outcome in my leadership depends upon my ability as a leader to develop and equip those closest to me. It also depends upon my ability to recognize the value that others bring to my organization. My goal is not to draw a following that results in a crowd. My goal is to develop leaders who become a movement.

Stop for a moment and think of the five or six people closest to you in your organization. Are you developing them? Do you have a game plan for their growth? Are they being properly equipped for leadership? Have they been able to lift your load?

Within my organization leadership development is continually emphasized. In their first training session, I give new leaders this principle: *As a potential leader you are either an asset or a liability to the organization.* I illustrate this truth by saying, "When there's a problem, a 'fire' in the organization, you as a leader are often the first to arrive at the scene. You have in your hands two buckets. One contains water and the other contains gasoline. The 'spark' before you will either become a greater problem because you pour the gasoline on it, or it will be extinguished because you use the bucket of water."

Every person within your organization also carries two

buckets. The question a leader needs to ask is, "Am I training them to use the gasoline or the water?"

AN ORGANIZATION'S GROWTH POTENTIAL IS DIRECTLY RELATED TO ITS PERSONNEL POTENTIAL

When conducting leadership conferences, I often make the statement, "Grow a leader—grow the organization." A company cannot grow without until its leaders grow within.

I am often amazed at the amount of money, energy, and marketing focus organizations spend on areas that will not produce growth. Why advertise that the customer is number one when the personnel have not been trained in customer service? When customers arrive, they will know the difference between an employee who has been trained to give service and one who hasn't. Slick brochures and catchy slogans will never overcome incompetent leadership.

In 1981 I became Senior Pastor of Skyline Wesleyan Church in San Diego, California. This congregation had averaged 1,000 in attendance from 1969 to 1981, and it was obviously on a plateau. When I assumed leadership responsibilities, the first question I asked was, "Why has the growth stopped?" I needed to find an answer, so I called my first staff meeting and gave a lecture titled *The Leadership Line*. My thesis was, "Leaders determine the level of an organization." I drew a line across a marker board and wrote the number

1,000. I shared with the staff that for thirteen years the average attendance at Skyline was 1,000. I knew the staff could lead 1,000 people effectively. What I did not know was whether they could lead 2,000 people. So I drew a dotted line and wrote the number 2,000, and I placed a question mark between the two lines. I then drew an arrow from the bottom 1,000 to the top 2,000 line and wrote the word "change."

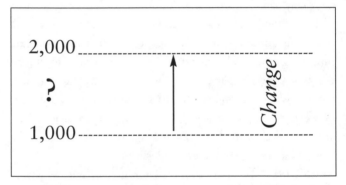

It would be my responsibility to equip them and help them make the necessary changes to reach our new goal. When the leaders changed positively, I knew the growth would come automatically. Now, I had to help them change themselves, or I knew I would literally have to change them by hiring others to take their places.

From 1981 to 1995 I gave this lecture at Skyline on three occasions. The last time, the number 4,000 was placed on the top line. As I discovered, the numbers changed, but the lecture didn't. The strength of any organization is a direct result of the strength of its leaders. Weak leaders equal weak organizations. Strong leaders equal strong organizations. Everything rises and falls on leadership.

Potential Leaders Help Carry the Load

Businessman Rolland Young said, "I am a self-made man, but I think if I had it to do over again, I would call in someone else!" Usually leaders fail to develop other leaders either because they lack training or because they possess wrong attitudes about allowing and encouraging others to come alongside them. Often, leaders wrongly believe that they must compete with the people close to them instead of working with them. Great leaders have a different mind-set. In *Profiles in Courage*, President John F. Kennedy wrote, "The best way to go along is to get along with others." This kind of positive interaction can happen only if the leader has an attitude of interdependency with others and is committed to win-win relationships.

EVERYTHING RISES AND FALLS ON LEADERSHIP.

Take a look at differences between the two views leaders possess about people:

Winning by Competitiveness	Winning by Cooperation
Look at others as enemies	Look at others as friends
Concentrate on yourself	Concentrate on others
Become suspicious of others	Become supportive of others
Win only if you are good	Win if you or others are good
Winning determined by your skills	Winning determined by the skills of many
Small victory	Large victory
Some joy	Much joy
There are winners and losers	There are only winners

Peter Drucker was correct when he said, "No executive has ever suffered because his people were strong and effective." The leaders around me lift my load in many ways. Here are two of the most important ones:

1. *They become a sounding board for me.* As a leader, I sometimes hear counsel that I don't want to hear but need to hear. That's the advantage of having leaders around you—having people who know how to make decisions. Followers tell you what you *want* to hear. Leaders tell you what you *need* to hear.

I have always encouraged those closest to me to give me advice on the front end. In other words, an opinion before a decision has potential value. An opinion after the decision has been made is worthless. Alex Agase, a college football coach, once said, "If you really want to give me advice, do it on Saturday afternoon between one and four o'clock, when you've got twenty-five seconds to do it, between plays. Don't give me advice on Monday. I know the right thing to do on Monday."

"No executive has ever suffered because his people were strong and effective."—Peter Drucker

---

2. They possess a leadership mind-set. Fellow leaders do more than work with the leader, they think like the leader. It gives them the power to lighten the load. This becomes invaluable in areas such as decision making, brainstorming, and providing security and direction to others.

A majority of my time is spent away from the office speaking at conferences and events. Therefore, it is essential that I have leaders in my organizations who can carry on effectively while I am gone. And they do. It happens because I have spent my life finding and developing potential leaders. The results are very gratifying.

Leaders Attract Potential Leaders

Birds of a feather really do flock together. I really believe that it takes a leader to know a leader, grow a leader, and show a leader. I have also found that it takes a leader to attract a leader.

Attraction is the obvious first step to equipping others, yet I find many people in leadership positions who are unable to accomplish this task. Good leaders are able to attract potential leaders because:

- Leaders think like them.

- Leaders express feelings that other leaders sense.

- Leaders create an environment that attracts potential leaders.

- Leaders are not threatened by people with great potential.

For example, a person in a leadership position who is a "5" on a scale of 1 to 10 will not attract a leader who is a "9." Why? Because leaders naturally size up any crowd and migrate to other leaders who are at the same or higher level.

Any leader who has only followers around him will be called upon to continually draw on his own resources to get things done. Without other leaders to carry the load, he will become fatigued and burnt out. Have you asked yourself lately, "Am I tired?" If the answer is yes, you may have a good reason for it, as this humorous story illustrates:

Somewhere in the world there is a country with a population of 220 million. Eighty-four million are over sixty years of age, which leaves 136 million to do the work. People under twenty years of age total 95 million, which leaves 41 million to do the work.

There are 22 million employed by the government, which leaves 19 million to do the work. Four million are in the Armed Forces, which leaves 15 million to do the work. Deduct 14,800,000, the number in state and city offices, and that leaves 200,000 to do the work. There are 188,000 in hospitals or insane asylums, so that leaves 12,000 to do the work.

It is of interest to note that in this country 11,998 people are in jail, so that leaves just two people to carry the load. That's you and me—and brother, I'm getting tired of doing everything myself!

Unless you want to carry the whole load yourself, you need to be developing and equipping leaders.

EQUIPPED LEADERS EXPAND AND ENHANCE THE FUTURE OF THE ORGANIZATION

One of the things my father taught me was the importance of people above all other elements in an organization. He was the president of a college for sixteen years. One day, as we sat on a campus bench, he explained that the most expensive workers on campus were not the highest paid. The most expensive ones were the people who were nonproductive. He explained that developing leaders took time and cost money. You usually had to pay leaders more. But such people were an invaluable asset. They attracted a higher quality of person; they were more productive; and they continued to add value to the organization. He closed the conversation by saying, "Most people produce only when they feel like it. Leaders produce even when they don't feel like it."

"Most people produce only when they feel like it.
Leaders produce even when they don't
feel like it."—Melvin Maxwell

The More People You Lead, the More Leaders You Need

Zig Ziglar says, "Success is the maximum utilization of the ability that you have." I believe a leader's success can be defined as *the maximum utilization of the abilities of those under him.* Andrew Carnegie explained it like this: "I wish to have as my epitaph: 'Here lies a man who was wise enough to bring into his service men who knew more than he.'" That is a worthy goal for any leader.

4

WHAT DOES A POTENTIAL
LEADER LOOK LIKE?

Great leaders seek out and find potential leaders,
then transform them into good leaders.

There is something much more important and scarce than ability: It is the ability to recognize ability. One of the primary responsibilities of a successful leader is to identify potential leaders. These are the people in whom you will want to invest your time equipping. Identifying them is not always an easy job, but it is critical.

Andrew Carnegie was a master at identifying potential leaders. Once asked by a reporter how he had managed to hire forty-three millionaires, Carnegie responded that the men had not been millionaires when they started working for him. They had become millionaires as a result. The reporter next wanted to know how he had developed these men to become such valuable leaders. Carnegie replied, "Men are developed the same way gold is mined. Several tons of dirt must be moved to get an ounce of gold. But you don't go into the mine looking for dirt," he added. "You go in looking for the gold." That's exactly the way to develop positive, successful people. Look for the gold, not the dirt; the good, not the bad. The more positive qualities you look for, the more you are going to find.

Selecting the Right Players

Professional sports organizations recognize the importance of selecting the right players. Every year, coaches and owners of professional baseball, basketball, and football teams look forward to the draft. To prepare for it, sports franchises spend much time and energy scouting new prospects. For instance, scouts from pro football organizations travel to regular-season college games, bowl games, senior-only bowl games, and camps to gain knowledge about prospective players. All of this enables the scouts to bring plenty of information back to the owners and head coaches so that when draft day arrives, the teams can pick the most promising players. Team owners and coaches know that the future success of their teams depends largely on their ability to draft effectively.

It's no different in business. You must select the right players in your organization. If you select well, the benefits are multiplied and seem nearly endless. If you select poorly, the problems are multiplied and seem endless.

The key to making the right choice depends on two things:

(1) your ability to see the big picture, and (2) your ability to judge potential employees during the selection process.

It is a good idea to start with an inventory. I use this one because I always want to look inside as well as outside the organization to find candidates. I call this list the Five A's:

Assessment of needs:	What is needed?
Assets on hand:	Who in the organization is available?
Ability of candidates:	Who is able?
Attitude of candidates:	Who is willing?
Accomplishments of candidates:	Who gets things done?

Notice that the inventory begins with an assessment of needs. The leader of the organization must base that assessment on the big picture. While he was manager of the Chicago Cubs, Charlie Grimm reportedly received a phone call from one of his scouts. The man was excited and began to shout over the telephone, "Charlie, I've landed the greatest young pitcher in the land! He struck out every man who came to bat. Twenty-seven in a row. Nobody even hit a foul until the ninth inning. The pitcher is right here with me. What shall I do?" Charlie replied, "Sign up the guy who got the foul. We're looking for hitters." Charlie knew what the team needed.

There is one situation that supersedes a needs analysis:

When a truly exceptional person is available but doesn't necessarily match the current need, do whatever you can to hire him or her anyway. In the long run, that person will positively impact the organization. You see this kind of decision making in sports. Football coaches generally draft players to fill specific needs. If they lack a strong running back, they draft the best running back available. But sometimes they get an opportunity to draft an "impact player," a superstar who can instantly change the whole complexion of the team. Incidentally, impact players usually possess not only athletic ability but also leadership skills. Even as rookies, they have all the qualities to be team captains. When I have an opportunity to hire someone who is exceptional—a superstar—I do it. Then I find a place for him or her. Good people are hard to find, and there is always room for one more productive person in an organization.

Qualities to Look for in a Leader

To find leaders to equip, you first need to know what they look like. Here are ten leadership qualities to seek in anyone you hire:

1. Character

The first thing to look for in any kind of leader or potential leader is strength of character. I have found nothing more important than this quality. Serious character flaws cannot be ignored. They will eventually make a leader ineffective—every time.

Character flaws should not be confused with weaknesses. We all have weaknesses. They can be overcome through training or experience. Character flaws cannot be changed overnight. Change usually takes a long period of time and involves significant relational investment and dedication on the part of the leader. Any person that you hire who has character flaws will be the weak link in your organization. Depending on the nature of the character flaw, the person has the potential to destroy the organization.

Some of the qualities that make up good character include: honesty, integrity, self-discipline, teachability, dependability, perseverance, conscientiousness, and a strong work ethic. The words of a person with right character match the deeds. His reputation is solid. His manner is straightforward.

The assessment of character can be difficult. Warning signs to watch for include:

- A person's failure to take responsibility for his actions or circumstances

- Unfulfilled promises or obligations

- Failure to meet deadlines

You can tell much about a person's ability to lead others from how well he manages his own life. Look at his interaction with others too. You can tell much about a person's character from his relationships. Examine his relationships with superiors, colleagues, and subordinates. Talk to your employees to find out how the potential leader treats them. This will give you additional insight.

LEADERSHIP IS INFLUENCE.

---

2. INFLUENCE

Leadership is influence. Every leader has these two characteristics: (A) he is going somewhere; and (B) he is able to persuade others to go with him. Influence by itself is not enough. That influence must be measured to determine its *quality*. When looking at a potential leader's influence, examine the following:

What is the leader's level of influence? Does that person have followers due to position (he uses the power of his job title), permission (he has developed relationships which motivate), production (he and his followers consistently produce results), personnel development (he has developed others around him), or personhood (he transcends the organization and develops people on a world-class scale)?

Who influences the leader? Who is she following? People become like their models. Is her model ethical? Does her model have the right priorities?

Whom does he influence? Likewise, the quality of the follower will indicate the quality of the leader. Are his followers positive producers or a bunch of mediocre yes-men?

Stuart Briscoe, in *Discipleship for Ordinary People*, tells the story of a young clergyman who officiated at the funeral of a war veteran. The veteran's military friends wanted to participate in the service to honor their comrade, so they requested that the young pastor lead them down to the casket for a moment of remembrance and then out through a side door. The occasion failed to have the desired effect when the clergyman led them through the wrong door. In full view of the other mourners, the men marched with military precision into a broom closet and had to beat a hasty and confused retreat. Every leader must know where he is going. And every follower had better be sure he's behind a leader who knows what he's doing.

3. Positive Attitude

A positive attitude is one of the most valuable assets a person can have in life. My belief in this is so strong that I wrote an entire book on the subject, *The Winning Attitude: Your Key to Personal Success*. So often, what people say their problem is really isn't their problem. Their problem is the attitude that causes them to handle life's obstacles poorly.

The individual whose attitude causes him to approach life from an entirely positive perspective is someone who can be called a no-limit person. In other words, the person doesn't accept the normal limitations of life as most people do. He is determined to walk to the very edge of his potential, or his product's potential, before he accepts defeat. People with positive attitudes are able to go places where others can't. They do things that others can't. They are not restricted by self-imposed limitations.

A person with a positive attitude is like a bumblebee. The bumblebee should not be able to fly, because the size, weight, and shape of its body in relationship to its wingspread makes flying aerodynamically impossible. But the bumblebee, being ignorant of scientific theory, flies anyway and makes honey every day.

This no-limit mind-set allows a person to start each day with a positive disposition, as did an elevator operator I once read about. One Monday morning, in a full elevator, the man began humming a tune. One passenger, irritated by the man's mood, snapped, "What are you so happy about?" "Well, sir," replied the operator happily, "I ain't never lived this day before." Not only does the future look bright when the attitude is right, but the present is much more enjoyable too. The positive person understands that the journey is as enjoyable as the destination.

Think of the attitude like this:

> It is the advance man of our true selves.
> Its roots are inward but its fruit is outward.
> It is our best friend or our worst enemy.
> It is more honest and more consistent than our words.
> It is an outward look based on past experiences.
> It is a thing which draws people to us or repels them.
> It is never content until it is expressed.
> It is the librarian of our past.
> It is the speaker of our present.
> It is the prophet of our future.[1]

Attitude sets the tone, not only for the leader with the attitude, but for the people following him or her.

4. EXCELLENT PEOPLE SKILLS

A leader without people skills soon has no followers. Andrew Carnegie, a fantastic leader, is reported to have paid Charles Schwab a salary of $1 million a year simply because of his excellent people skills. Carnegie had other leaders who understood the job better and whose experience and training were better suited to the work. But they lacked the essential human quality of being able to get others to help them, and Schwab could get the best out of his fellow workers. People may admire a person who has only talent and ability, but they will not follow him—not for long.

Excellent people skills involve a genuine concern for others, the ability to understand people, and the decision to make positive interaction with others a primary concern. Our behavior toward others determines their behavior toward us. A successful leader knows this.

5. EVIDENT GIFTS

Every person God creates has gifts. One of our jobs as leaders is to make an assessment of those gifts when considering a person for employment or for equipping. I think of every job candidate as a "wanna be" leader. My observation is that there are four types of wanna-bes:

Never be. Some people simply lack the ability to do a particular job. They simply are not gifted for the particular task at hand. A *never be* who is directed into an area where he is not gifted becomes frustrated, often blames others for his lack of success, and eventually burns out. Redirected, he has a chance of reaching his potential.

Could be. A *could be* is a person with the right gifts and abilities but lacking self-discipline. She may even be a person with superstar abilities who just can't get herself to perform. This person needs to develop the self-discipline to "just do it."

Should be. A *should be* is someone with raw talent (gifts) but few skills for harnessing that ability. He needs training. Once he is given help in developing those skills, he will begin to become the person he was created to be.

Must be. The only thing a *must be* lacks is opportunity. She has the right gifts, the right skills, and the right attitude. She has the drive to be the person she was created to be. It is up to you to be the leader who gives her that opportunity. If you don't, she will find someone else who will.

God creates all people with natural gifts. But He also makes them with two ends, one to sit on and one to think with. Success in life is dependent on which one of these ends is used the most, and it's a toss-up: Heads you win, and tails you lose!

6. Proven Track Record

Poet Archibald MacLeish once said, "There is only one thing more painful than learning from experience, and that is not learning from experience." Leaders who learn this truth develop successful track records over time. Everyone who breaks new ground, who strives to do something, makes mistakes. People without proven track records either haven't learned from their mistakes or haven't tried.

I've worked with many talented people who've established tremendous track records. When I first started my organization, one man stood out as a first-rate leader capable of the highest quality of leadership: Dick Peterson. He had worked with IBM for years, and he quickly demonstrated that experience had not been wasted on him. Dick already had a proven track record when I asked him to team with me in 1985 to start one of my companies, INJOY. In the beginning, we were long on potential and short on resources. Dick's hard work, planning, and insight turned a shoestring business operating out of his garage into an enterprise producing materials and influencing tens of thousands of leaders nationally and internationally every year. For fifteen years Dick served as the president of INJOY and helped get the company off the ground.

Management expert Robert Townsend notes, "Leaders come in all sizes, ages, shapes, and conditions. Some are poor administrators, some not overly bright. But there is one clue for spotting them. Since most people *per se* are mediocre, the true leader can be recognized because somehow or other, his people consistently turn in superior performances." Always check a candidate's past performance. A proven leader always has a proven track record.

7. Confidence

People will not follow a leader who does not have confidence in himself. In fact, people are naturally attracted to people who convey confidence. An excellent example can be seen in an incident in Russia during an attempted coup. Army tanks had surrounded the government building housing President Boris Yeltsin and his pro-democracy supporters. High-level military leaders had ordered the tank commander to open fire and kill Yeltsin. As the army rolled into position, Yeltsin strode from the building, climbed up on a tank, looked the commander in the eye, and thanked him for coming over to the side of democracy. Later the commander admitted that they had not intended to go over to his side. Yeltsin had appeared so confident and commanding that the soldiers talked after he left and decided to join him.

Confidence is characteristic of a positive attitude. The greatest achievers and leaders remain confident regardless of circumstances. Confidence is not simply for show. Confidence empowers. A *good* leader has the ability to instill within his people confidence in himself. A *great* leader has the ability to instill within his people confidence in themselves.

8. Self-Discipline

Great leaders always have self-discipline—without exception. Unfortunately, our society seeks instant gratification rather than self-discipline. We want instant breakfast, fast food, movies on demand, and quick cash from ATMs. But success doesn't come instantly. Neither does the ability to lead. As General Dwight D. Eisenhower said, "There are no victories at bargain prices."

Because we live in a society of instant gratification, we cannot take for granted that the potential leaders we interview will have self-discipline—that they will be willing to pay the price of great leadership. When it comes to self-discipline, people choose one of two things: the pain of discipline that comes from sacrifice and growth, or the pain of regret that comes from the easy road and missed opportunities. Each person in life chooses. In *Adventures in Achievement*, E. James Rohn says that the pain of discipline weighs ounces. Regret weighs tons.

There are two areas of self-discipline we must look for in potential leaders we are considering equipping. The first is in the emotions. Effective leaders recognize that their emotional reactions are their own responsibility. A leader who decides not to allow other people's actions to dictate his reactions experiences an empowering freedom. As the Greek philosopher Epictetus said, "No person is free who is not master of himself."

The second area concerns time. Every person on the planet is given the same allotment of minutes in a day. But each person's level of self-discipline dictates how effectively those minutes are used. Disciplined people are always growing, always striving for improvement, and they maximize the use of their time. I have found three things that characterize disciplined leaders:

- They have identified specific long- and short-term goals for themselves.

- They have a plan for achieving those goals.

- They have a desire that motivates them to continue working to accomplish those goals.

Progress comes at a price. When you interview a potential leader, determine whether he or she is willing to pay the price. The author of the popular cartoon comic strip *Ziggy* recognized this when he drew the following scene:

As our friend Ziggy, in his little automobile, drove down a road, he saw two signs. The first stated in bold letters, THE ROAD TO SUCCESS. Farther down the road stood the second sign. It read, PREPARE TO STOP FOR TOLLS.

9. EFFECTIVE COMMUNICATION SKILLS

Never underestimate the importance of communication. It consumes enormous amounts of our time. One study, reported by D. K. Burlow in *The Process of Communication*, states that the average American spends 70 percent of his active hours each day communicating verbally. Without the ability to communicate, a leader cannot effectively cast his vision and call his people to act on that vision.

A leader's ability to convey confidence and his ability to communicate effectively are similar. Both require action on his part and a response from the follower. Communication is positive *interaction*. When communication is one-sided, it can be comical. You may have heard the story of the frustrated judge preparing to hear a divorce case:

> "Why do you want a divorce?" the judge asked. "On what grounds?"
>
> "All over. We have an acre and a half," responded the woman.
>
> "No, no," said the judge. "Do you have a grudge?"
>
> "Yes, sir. Fits two cars."
>
> "I need a reason for the divorce," said the judge impatiently. "Does he beat you up?"
>
> "Oh, no. I'm up at six every day to do my exercises. He gets up later."
>
> "Please," said the exasperated judge. "What is the reason you want a divorce?"
>
> "Oh," she replied. "We can't seem to communicate with each other."

When I look at a potential leader's communication skills, I look for the following:

A genuine concern for the person he's talking to. When people sense that you have a concern for them, they are willing to listen to what you have to say. Liking people is the beginning of the ability to communicate.

The ability to focus on the responder. Poor communicators are focused on themselves and their own opinions. Good communicators focus on the response of the person they're talking to. Good communicators also read body language.

The ability to communicate with all kinds of people. A good communicator has the ability to set a person at ease. She can find a way to relate to nearly anyone of any background.

Eye contact with the person he's speaking to. Most people who are being straight with you are willing to look you in the eye.

A warm smile. The fastest way to open the lines of communication is to smile. A smile overcomes innumerable communication barriers, crossing the boundaries of culture, race, age, class, gender, education, and economic status.

If I expect a person to lead, I must also expect him to be able to communicate.

10. Discontent with the Status Quo

I've told my staff before that *status quo* is Latin for "the mess we're in." Leaders see what is, but more important, they have vision for what could be. They are never content with things as they are. To be leading, by definition, is to be in front, breaking new ground, conquering new worlds, moving away from the status quo. Donna Harrison states, "Great leaders are never satisfied with current levels of performance. They constantly strive for higher and higher levels of achievement." They move beyond the status quo themselves, and they ask the same of those around them.

Dissatisfaction with the status quo does not mean a negative attitude or grumbling. It has to do with willingness to be different and take risks. A person who refuses to risk change fails to grow. A leader who loves the status quo soon becomes a follower. Raymond Smith, former CEO and Chairman of the Bell Atlantic Corporation, once remarked, "Taking the safe road, doing your job, and not making any waves may not get you fired (right away, at least), but it sure won't do much for your career or your company over the long haul. We're not dumb. We know that administrators are easy to find and cheap to keep. Leaders—risk takers—are in very short supply. And ones with vision are pure gold."

Risk seems dangerous to people more comfortable with old problems than new solutions. The difference between the energy and time that it takes to put up with the old problems and the energy and time it takes to come up with new solutions is surprisingly small. The difference is attitude. When seeking potential leaders, seek people who seek solutions.

Good leaders deliberately seek out and find potential leaders. Great leaders not only find them, but transform them into other great leaders. They have an ability to recognize ability and a strategy for finding leaders who make it happen. That's what takes their organizations to the next level.

5

WHAT DOES IT TAKE TO EQUIP A LEADER?

Equipping, like nurturing, is an ongoing process.

Equipping is similar to training. But I prefer the term "equipping" because it more accurately describes the process potential leaders must go through. Training is generally focused on specific job tasks; for instance, you train a person to use a copy machine or to answer a phone in a particular way. Training is only a part of the equipping process that prepares a person for leadership.

When I think of equipping a potential leader, I think of preparing an unskilled person to scale a tall mountain peak. His preparation is a process. Certainly he needs to be outfitted with equipment, such as cold-weather clothing, ropes, picks, and spikes. He also needs to be trained how to use that equipment.

A mountain climber's preparation, though, involves much more than simply having the correct equipment and knowing how to use it. The person must be conditioned physically to prepare him for the difficult climb. He must be trained to be a part of a team. Most important, he must be taught to *think* like a mountain climber. He needs to be able to look at a peak and *see* how it is to be conquered. Without going through the complete equipping process, he not only won't make it to the top of the mountain, but he also might find himself stranded on the side of the mountain, freezing to death.

Equipping, like nurturing, is an ongoing process. You don't equip a person in a few hours or a day. And it can't be done using a formula or a videotape. Equipping must be tailored to each potential leader.

EQUIPPING IS AN ONGOING PROCESS.

YOUR ROLE AS EQUIPPER

The ideal equipper is a person who can impart the vision of the work, evaluate the potential leader, give him the tools he needs, and then help him along the way at the beginning of his journey.

The equipper is a *model*—a leader who does the job, does it well, does it right, and does it with consistency.

The equipper is a *mentor*—an advisor who has the vision of the organization and can communicate it to others. He or she has experience to draw upon.

The equipper is an *empowerer*—one who can instill in the potential leader the desire and ability to do the work. He or she is able to lead, teach, and assess the progress of the person being equipped.

The steps that follow will take you through the whole process. They begin with building a relationship with your potential leaders. From that foundation, you can build a program for their development, supervise their progress, empower them to do the job, and finally get them to pass on the legacy.

Develop a Personal Relationship with the People You Equip

All good mentoring relationships begin with personal relationships. As your people get to know and like you, their desire to follow your direction and learn from you will increase. If they don't like you, they will not want to learn from you, and the equipping process slows down or even stops.

To build relationships, begin by listening to people's life stories, their journeys so far. Your genuine interest in them will mean a lot to them. It will also help you to know their personal strengths and weaknesses. Ask them about their goals and what motivates them. Find out what kind of temperament they have. If you first find their hearts, they'll be glad to give you their hands.

ALL GOOD MENTORING RELATIONSHIPS BEGIN
WITH PERSONAL RELATIONSHIPS.

Share Your Dream

While getting to know your people, share your dream. It helps them to know you and where you're going. There's no act that will better show them your heart and your motivation.

Woodrow Wilson once said, "We grow by dreams. All big individuals are dreamers. They see things in the soft haze of a spring day, or in the red fire on a long winter's evening. Some of us let those great dreams die, but others nourish and protect them; nourish them through bad days until they bring them to the sunshine and light which comes always to those who sincerely hope that their dreams will come true." I have often wondered, "Does the person make the dream or does the dream make the person?" My conclusion is both are equally true.

All good leaders have a dream. All great leaders share their dream with others who can help them make it a reality. As Florence Littauer suggests, we must

Dare to dream: Have the desire to do something bigger than yourself.

Prepare the dream: Do your homework; be ready when the opportunity comes.

Wear the dream: Do it.

Share the dream: Make others a part of the dream, and it will become even greater than you had hoped.

ASK FOR COMMITMENT

In his book *The One Minute Manager*, Ken Blanchard says, "There's a difference between interest and commitment. When you are interested in doing something, you do it only when it is convenient. When you are committed to something, you accept no excuses." Don't equip people who are merely interested. Equip the ones who are committed.

To determine whether your people are committed, first you must make sure they know what it will cost them to become leaders. That means that you must be sure not to undersell the job—let them know what it's going to take. If they won't commit, don't go any further in the equipping process. Don't waste your time.

SET GOALS FOR GROWTH

People need clear objectives set before them if they are to achieve anything of value. Success never comes instantaneously. It comes from taking many small steps. A set of goals becomes a map a potential leader can follow in order to grow. As Shad Helmsetter states in *You Can Excel in Time of Change*, "It is the goal that shapes the plan; it is the plan that sets the action; it is the action that achieves the result; and it is the result that brings the success. And it all begins with the simple word *goal.*" We, as equipping leaders, must introduce our people to the practice of setting and achieving goals.

When you help your people set goals, use the following guidelines:

Make the goals appropriate. Always keep in mind the job you want the people to do and the desired result: the development of your people into effective leaders. Identify goals that will contribute to that larger goal.

Make the goals attainable. Nothing will make people want to quit faster than facing unachievable goals. I like the comment made by Ian MacGregor, former AMAX Corporation chairman of the board: "I work on the same principle as people who train horses. You start with low fences, easily achieved goals, and work up. It's important in management never to ask people to try to accomplish goals they can't accept."

Make the goals measurable. Your potential leaders will never know when they have achieved their goals if they aren't measurable. When they are measurable, the knowledge that they have been attained will give them a sense of accomplishment. It will also free them to set new goals in place of the old ones.

Clearly state the goal. When goals have no clear focus, neither will the actions of the people trying to achieve them.

Make the goals require a "stretch." As I mentioned before, goals have to be achievable. On the other hand, when goals don't require a stretch, the people achieving them won't grow. The leader must know his people well enough to identify attainable goals that require a stretch.

Put the goals in writing. When people write down their goals, it makes them more accountable for those goals. A study of a Yale University graduating class showed that the small percentage of graduates who had written down their goals accomplished more than all of the other graduates combined. Putting goals in writing works.

COMMUNICATE THE FUNDAMENTALS

For people to be productive and satisfied professionally, they have to know what their fundamental responsibilities are. It sounds so simple, but Peter Drucker says one of the critical problems in the workplace today is that there is a lack of understanding between the employer and employee as to what the employee is to do. Often employees are made to feel they are vaguely responsible for everything. It paralyzes them. Instead, we need to make clear to them what they *are* and *are not* responsible for. Then they will be able to focus their efforts on what we want, and they will succeed.

Look again at how a basketball team works. Each of the five players has a particular job. There is a shooting guard whose job is to score points. The other guard is a point guard. His job is to pass the ball to people who can score. Another player is a power forward who is expected to get rebounds. The small forward's job is to score. The center is supposed to rebound, block shots, and score. Each person on the team knows what his job is, what his unique contribution to the team must be. When each concentrates on his particular responsibilities, the team can win.

Finally, a leader must communicate to his or her people that their work has value to the organization and to the individual leader. To the employee, this often is the most important fundamental of all.

PERFORM THE FIVE-STEP PROCESS OF TRAINING PEOPLE

Part of the equipping process includes training people to perform the specific tasks of the jobs they are to do. The approach the leader takes to training will largely determine his people's success or failure. If he takes a dry, academic approach, the potential leaders will remember little of what's taught.

The best type of training takes advantage of the way

people learn. Researchers tell us that we remember 10 percent of what we hear, 50 percent of what we see, 70 percent of what we say, and 90 percent of what we hear, see, say, and do. Knowing that, we have to develop an approach to how we will train. I have found the best training method to be a five-step process:

Step 1: I model. The process begins with my doing the tasks while the people being trained watch. When I do this, I try to give them an opportunity to see me go through the whole process.

Step 2: I mentor. During this next step, I continue to perform the task, but this time the person I'm training comes alongside me and assists in the process. I also take time to explain not only the *how* but also the *why* of each step.

Step 3: I monitor. We exchange places this time. The trainee performs the task and I assist and correct. It's especially important during this phase to be positive and encouraging to the trainee. It keeps him trying and it makes him want to improve rather than give up. Work with him until he develops consistency. Once he's gotten down the process, ask him to explain it to you. It will help him to understand and remember.

Step 4: I motivate. I take myself out of the task at this point and let the trainee go. My task is to make sure he knows how to do it without help and to keep encouraging him so he will continue to improve. It is important for me to stay with him until he senses success. It's a great motivator. At this time the trainee may want to make improvements to the process. Encourage him to do it, and at the same time learn from him.

Step 5: I multiply. This is my favorite part of the whole process. Once the new leaders do the job well, it becomes their turn to teach others how to do it. As teachers know, the best way to learn something is to teach it. And the beauty of this is it frees me to do other important developmental tasks while others carry on the training.

GIVE THE "BIG THREE"

All the training in the world will provide limited success if you don't turn your people loose to do the job. I believe that if I get the best people, give them my vision, train them in the basics, and then let go, I will get a high return from them. As General George S. Patton once remarked, "Never tell people how to do things. Tell them what to do and they will surprise you with their ingenuity."

You can't turn people loose without structure, but you also want to give them enough freedom to be creative. The way to do that is to give them the big three: *responsibility, authority,* and *accountability.*

What is difficult for some leaders is allowing their people to keep the responsibility after it's been given. Poor managers want to control every detail of their people's work. When that happens, the potential leaders who work for them become frustrated and don't develop. Rather than desiring more responsibility, they become indifferent or avoid responsibility altogether. If you want your people to take responsibility, truly give it to them.

With responsibility must go authority. Progress does not come unless they are given together. Winston Churchill, while addressing the House of Commons during the Second World War, said, "I am your servant. You have the right to dismiss me when you please. What you have no right to do is ask me to bear responsibility without the power of action." When responsibility and authority come together, people become genuinely empowered.

There's an important aspect of authority that needs to be noted. When we first give authority to new leaders, we are actually *giving them permission* to have authority rather than *giving them authority* itself. True authority has to be earned.

We must give our people permission to develop authority. That is our responsibility. They, in turn, must take responsibility for earning it.

I have found there are different levels of authority:

Position. The most basic kind of authority comes from a person's position on the organizational chart. This type of authority does not extend beyond the parameters of the job description. This is where all new leaders start. From here they may either earn greater authority, or they can minimize what little authority they have been given. It's up to them.

Competence. This type of authority is based on a person's professional capabilities, the ability to do a job. Followers give competent leaders authority within their area of expertise.

Personality. Followers will also give authority to people based on their personal characteristics, such as personality, appearance, and charisma. Authority based on personality is a little broader than competence-based authority, but it is not really more advanced because it tends to be superficial.

Integrity. Authority based on integrity comes from a person's core. It is based on character. When new leaders gain authority based on their integrity, they have crossed into a new stage of their development.

Spirituality. In secular circles, people rarely consider the power of spiritual-based authority. It comes from people's individual experiences with God and from His power working through them. It is the highest form of authority.

Leaders must earn authority with each new group of people. However, I have found that once leaders have gained authority on a particular level, it takes very little time for them to establish that level of authority with another group of people. The higher the level of authority, the more quickly it happens.

Once responsibility and authority have been given to people, they are empowered to make things happen. But we also have to be sure they are making the right things happen. That's where accountability comes into the picture. If we are providing them the right climate, our people will not fear accountability. They will admit mistakes and see them as a part of the learning process.

The leader's part of accountability involves taking the time to review the new leader's work and give honest, constructive criticism. It is crucial that the leader be supportive but honest. It's been said that when Harry Truman was thrust into the presidency upon the death of President Franklin D. Roosevelt, Speaker of the House Sam Rayburn gave him some fatherly advice: "From here on out you're going to have lots of people around you. They'll try to put a wall around you and cut you off from any ideas but theirs. They'll tell you what a great man you are, Harry. But you and I both know you ain't." Rayburn was holding President Truman accountable.

Give Them the Tools They Need

Giving responsibility without resources is ridiculous; it is incredibly limiting. Abraham Maslow said, "If the only tool you have is a hammer, you tend to see every problem as a nail." If we want our people to be creative and resourceful, we need to provide resources.

Obviously, the most basic tools are pieces of equipment, such as copying machines, computers, and whatever else simplifies someone's work. We must be sure not only to provide everything necessary for a job to be done, but also equipment that will allow jobs, especially "B" priorities, to be done more quickly and efficiently. Always work toward freeing people's time for important things.

Tools, however, include much more than equipment. It is important to provide developmental tools. Spend time mentoring people in specific areas of need. Be willing to spend money on things like books, tapes, seminars, and professional conferences. There is a wealth of good information out there, and fresh ideas from outside an organization can stimulate growth. Be creative in providing tools. It will keep your people growing and equip them to do the job well.

Check on Them Systematically

I believe in touching base with people frequently. I like to give mini-evaluations all the time. Leaders who wait to give feedback only during annual formal evaluations are asking for trouble. People need the encouragement of being told they're doing well on a regular basis. They also need to hear as soon as possible when they are not doing well. It prevents a lot of problems with the organization, and it improves the leader.

How often I check on people is determined by a number of factors:

The importance of the task. When something is critical to the success of the organization, I touch base often.

The demands of the work. I find that if the work is very demanding, the person performing it needs encouragement more often.

The newness of the work. Some leaders have no problem tackling a new task, no matter how different it is from previous work. Others have great difficulty adapting. I check often on the people who are less flexible or creative.

The newness of the worker. I want to give new leaders every possible chance to succeed. So I check on newer people more often. That way I can help them anticipate problems and make sure that they have a series of successes. By that they gain confidence.

The responsibility of the worker. When I know I can give a person a task and it will always get done, I may not check on that person until the task is complete. With less responsible people, I can't afford to do that.

My approach to checking on people also varies from person to person. For instance, rookies and veterans should be treated differently. But no matter how long people have been with me, there are some things I always do: Discuss feelings; measure progress; give feedback; and give encouragement.

Though it doesn't happen very often, I occasionally have a person whose progress is repeatedly poor. When that happens, I try to determine what's gone wrong. Usually poor performance is a result of one of three things: (1) a mismatch between the job and the person; (2) inadequate training or leadership; or (3) deficiencies in the person performing the work. Before I take any action, I always try to determine what the issues are. I line up my facts to be sure there really is a deficiency in performance and not just a problem with my perception. Next I define as precisely as possible what the deficiency is. Finally, I check with the person who is not performing to get the other side of the story.

Once I've done my homework, I try to determine where the deficiency is. If it's a mismatch, I explain the problem to the person, move him to a place that fits, and reassure him of my confidence in him.

If the problem involves training or leadership issues, I back up and redo whatever step hasn't been performed properly. Once again, I let the person know what the problem was and give him plenty of encouragement.

If the problem is with the person, I sit down with him and let him know about it. I make it clear where his failures are and what he must do to overcome them. Then I give him another chance. But I also begin the documentation process in case I have to fire him. I want him to succeed, but I will waste no time letting him go if he doesn't do what it takes to improve.

Conduct Periodic Equipping Meetings

Even after you've completed most of your people's training and are preparing to take them into their next growth phase—development—continue to conduct periodic equipping meetings. It helps your people stay on track, helps them keep growing, and encourages them to begin taking responsibility for equipping themselves.

When I prepare an equipping meeting, I include the following:

Good news. I always start on a positive note. I review the good things that are happening in the organization and pay particular attention to their areas of interest and responsibility.

Vision. People can get so caught up in their day-to-day responsibilities that they lose sight of the vision that drives the organization. Use the opportunity of an equipping meeting to recast that vision.

Content. Content will depend on their needs. Try to focus training on areas that will help them in the priority areas, and orient the training on the people, not the lesson.

Administration. Cover any organizational items that give the people a sense of security and encourage their leadership.

Empowerment. Take time to connect with the people you

equip. Encourage them personally. And show them how the equipping session empowers them to perform their jobs better. They will leave the meeting feeling positive and ready to work.

The entire equipping process takes a lot of time and attention. It requires more time and dedication from the equipping leader than mere training. But its focus is long term, not short term. Rather than creating followers or even adding new leaders, it *multiplies* leaders. As I explained earlier, it is not complete until the equipper and the new leader select someone for the new leader to train. It is only then that the equipping process has come full circle. Without a successor, there can be no success.

PART III

EQUIPPING FOR THE NEXT LEVEL

6

HOW CAN A LEADER
INSPIRE OTHERS TO EXCEL?

Adding value is really the essence of equipping others.

In 1296, King Edward I of England assembled a large army and crossed the border of his own nation into Scotland. Edward was a skilled leader and fierce warrior. A tall, strong man, he had gained his first real combat experience beginning at age twenty-five. In the following years, he became a seasoned veteran while fighting in the Crusades in the Holy Lands.

At age fifty-seven, he was fresh from victories in Wales, whose people he'd crushed and whose land he'd annexed. In that conflict, his purpose had been clear: He said it was "to check the impetuous rashness of the Welsh, to punish their presumption and to wage war against them to their extermination."[1]

Edward's invasion of Scotland was intended to break the will of the Scottish people once and for all. Previously, he had managed to make himself overlord of the territory and then placed a weak king over it, a man the people of Scotland called Toom Tabard, meaning "empty coat." Then Edward bullied the straw king until he rebelled, thus giving the English monarch a reason to invade the country. The Scottish people crumpled.

A BOLD LEADER EMERGED

Edward sacked the castle of Berwick and massacred its inhabitants. Other castles surrendered in quick succession. The Scottish king was stripped of power, and many believed that the fate of the Scots would be the same as that of the Welsh. But they didn't take into account the efforts of one man: Sir William Wallace, who is still revered as a national hero in Scotland even though he has been dead for nearly seven hundred years.

If you saw the movie *Braveheart,* then you have an image of William Wallace as a fierce and determined fighter who valued freedom above all else. His older brother, Malcolm, as the firstborn son, was expected to follow in the footsteps of their father as a warrior. William, as many second sons of the day, was instead groomed for the clergy. He was taught to value ideas, including freedom. But Wallace grew to resent the oppressive English rulers after his father was killed in an ambush and his mother was forced to live in exile. At age nineteen, he became a fighter when a group of Englishmen tried to bully him. By his early twenties, William Wallace was a highly skilled warrior.

THE PEOPLE WENT TO A HIGHER LEVEL

During the time of William Wallace and Edward I, warfare was usually conducted by trained knights, professional soldiers, and sometimes hired mercenaries. The larger and more seasoned the army, the greater their power. When Edward faced the smaller Welsh army, they didn't stand a chance. And the same was expected of the Scots. But Wallace had an unusual ability. He drew the common people of Scotland to him, he made them believe in the cause of freedom, and he inspired and equipped them to fight against the professional war machine of England. He enlarged their vision and their abilities.

William Wallace was ultimately unable to defeat the English and gain Scotland's independence. At age thirty-three, he was brutally executed. (His treatment was actually worse than that portrayed in the movie *Braveheart.*) But his legacy of enlargement carried on. The next year, inspired by Wallace's example, nobleman Robert Bruce claimed the throne of Scotland and rallied not only the peasants but also the nobility. And in 1314, Scotland finally gained its hard-fought independence.

Characteristics of Enlarging Leaders

Team members always love and admire a player who is able to help them go to another level, someone who enlarges them and empowers them to be successful. Those kinds of people are like the Boston Celtics Hall of Fame center Bill Russell, who said, "The most important measure of how good a game I played was how much better I'd made my teammates play."

Leaders who enlarge their teammates have several things in common:

They Value Their Team Members

Industrialist Charles Schwab observed, "I have yet to find the man, however exalted his station, who did not do better work and put forth greater effort under a spirit of approval than under a spirit of criticism." Your team members can tell whether you believe in them. People's performances usually reflect the expectations of those they respect.

"THE MOST IMPORTANT MEASURE OF HOW GOOD A GAME
I PLAYED WAS HOW MUCH BETTER I'D MADE
MY TEAMMATES PLAY."—BILL RUSSELL

They Value What Their Team Members Value

Players who enlarge others do more than value their fellow team members; they understand what their team members value. They listen to discover what they talk about and watch to see what they spend their money on. That kind of knowledge, along with a desire to relate to their fellow players, creates a strong connection between them. And it makes possible an enlarger's next characteristic.

They Add Value to Their Team Members

Adding value is really the essence of enlarging others. It's finding ways to help others improve their abilities and attitudes. A leader who equips and enlarges others looks for the gifts, talents, and uniqueness in other people, and then helps them to increase those abilities for their benefit and for that of the entire team. An enlarging leader is able to take others to a whole new level.

They Make Themselves More Valuable

Enlargers work to make themselves better, not only because it benefits them personally, but also because it helps them to help others. You cannot give what you do not have. If you want to increase the ability of your team members, make yourself better.

HOW TO BECOME AN ENLARGER

If you want to be an enlarging team leader, then do the following:

1. BELIEVE IN OTHERS BEFORE THEY BELIEVE IN YOU

If you want to help people become better, you need to become an initiator. You can't hold back. Ask yourself, What is special, unique, and wonderful about that team member? Then share your observations with the person and with others. If you believe in others and give them a positive reputation to uphold, you can help them to become better than they think they are.

2. SERVE OTHERS BEFORE THEY SERVE YOU

One of the most beneficial services you can perform is helping other human beings to reach their potential. In your family, serve your spouse. In business, help your colleagues to shine. And whenever possible, give credit to others for the team's success.

3. ADD VALUE TO OTHERS BEFORE THEY ADD VALUE TO YOU

A basic truth of life is that people will always move toward anyone who increases them and away from others who devalue them. You can enlarge others by pointing out their strengths and helping them to focus on improvement.

For as long as he could remember, a boy named Chris Greicius dreamed of someday becoming a police officer. But there was a major obstacle standing in his way. He had leukemia, and he was not expected to make it to adulthood. When he was seven years old, Chris's battle with the disease took a turn for the worse, and that's when a family friend, who was a U.S. customs officer, arranged for Chris to come as close as he could to living his dream. He made a call to Officer Ron Cox in Phoenix and arranged for Chris to spend the day with officers from the Arizona Department of Public Safety.

A BASIC TRUTH OF LIFE IS THAT PEOPLE WILL ALWAYS
MOVE TOWARD ANYONE WHO INCREASES THEM
AND AWAY FROM OTHERS WHO DEVALUE THEM.

When the day arrived, Chris was welcomed by three squad cars and a police motorcycle ridden by Frank Shankwitz. Then he was treated to a ride in a police helicopter. They finished the day by swearing Chris in as the first—and only—honorary state trooper. The next day, Cox enlisted the assistance of the company that manufactured the uniforms for the Arizona Highway Patrol, and within twenty-four hours, their people presented Chris with an official patrolman's uniform. He was ecstatic.

Two days later, Chris died in the hospital, his uniform close at hand. Officer Shankwitz was saddened by his little friend's death, but he was grateful that he had experienced the opportunity to help Chris. And he also realized that there were many children in circumstances similar to Chris's. That prompted Shankwitz to cofound the Make-A-Wish Foundation. In twenty years since then, he and his organization have enlarged the experiences of more than eighty thousand children.

There is nothing as valuable—or rewarding—as adding value to the lives of others. When you help others to go to another level, you go to another level yourself.

7

HOW CAN I HELP OTHERS FULFILL THEIR POTENTIAL?

*Having the right people
in the right places is essential to
individual and team success.*

If you succeed in developing people in your organization and equipping them to lead, you will be successful. If you enlarge them and motivate them to achieve, they will be grateful to you as their leader. And to be honest, you will have done more than many other leaders do. However, you can take yet another step that will help someone you equip to fulfill their potential. You can help them to find their niche in life. Good things happen when a player takes the place where he or she adds the most value. Great things happen when all the players on the team take the roles that maximize their strengths—their talent, skill, and experience. It takes every individual—and the whole team—to a whole new level.

When People Are in the Wrong Place

Just about everyone has experienced being on some kind of team where people had to take on roles that didn't suit them: an accountant forced to work with people all day, a basketball forward forced to play center, a guitarist filling in on keyboard, a teacher stuck doing paperwork, a spouse who hates the kitchen taking on the role of cook.

What happens to a team when one or more of its members constantly play "out of position"? First, morale erodes because the team isn't playing up to its capability. Then people become resentful. The people working in an area of weakness resent that their best is untapped. And other people on the team who know that they could better fill a mismatched position on the team resent that their skills are being overlooked. Before long, people become unwilling to work as a team. Then everyone's confidence begins to erode. And the situation just keeps getting worse. The team stops progressing, and the competition takes advantage of the team's obvious weaknesses. As a result, the team never realizes its potential. When people aren't where they do things well, things don't turn out well—for the individual or for the team.

Having the right people in the right places is essential to individual and team success. Take a look at how a team's dynamic changes according to the placement of people:

The Wrong Person in the Wrong Place = Regression

The Wrong Person in the Right Place = Frustration

The Right Person in the Wrong Place = Confusion

The Right Person in the Right Place = Progression

The Right People in the Right Places = Multiplication

It doesn't matter what kind of team you're dealing with: the principles are the same. David Ogilvy was right when he said, "A well-run restaurant is like a winning baseball team. It makes the most of every crew member's talent and takes advantage of every split-second opportunity to speed up service."

A few years ago I was asked to write a chapter for a book called *Destiny and Deliverance,* which was tied to the Dreamworks movie *The Prince of Egypt.* It was a wonderful experience, which I greatly enjoyed. During the writing process, I was invited to go to California and view parts of the movie while it was still in production. That made me want to do something I had never done before: attend a movie premiere in Hollywood.

My publisher managed to get me a pair of tickets for the premiere, and when the time arrived, my wife, Margaret, and I went out for the event. It was a blast. It was a high-energy event filled with movie stars and moviemakers. Margaret and I enjoyed the movie—and the whole experience—immensely.

Now, anybody who's gone to a movie, show, or sporting event with me knows my pattern. As soon as I am pretty certain about the outcome of a ball game, I hit the exit to beat the crowds. When the Broadway audience is giving the ovation, I'm gone. And the second the credits begin to roll in a movie, I'm out of my seat. As *The Prince of Egypt* came to a close, I started to get ready to get up, but not a person in the theater moved. And then something really surprising happened. As the credits rolled, people began to applaud the lesser known individuals whose names appeared on the screen: the costume designer, the gaffer, the key grip, the assistant director. It was a moment I'll never forget—and a great reminder that all players have a place where they add the most value. That not only helps people to reach their potential, but it builds the team. When each person does the job that's best for him or her, everybody wins.

TO PUT PEOPLE IN THEIR PLACE

NFL champion coach Vince Lombardi observed, "The achievements of an organization are the results of the combined effort of each individual." That is true, but creating a winning team doesn't come just from having the right individuals. Even if you have a great group of talented individuals, if each person is not doing what adds the most value to the team, you won't achieve your potential as a team. That's the art of leading a team. You've got to put people in their place—and I mean that in the most positive way!

To take people to the next level by putting them in the places that utilize their talents and maximize the team's potential, you need three things. You must . . .

1. Know the Team

You cannot build a winning team or organization if you don't know its vision, purpose, culture, or history. If you don't know where the team is trying to go—and why it's trying to get there—you cannot bring the team to the height of its potential. You've got to start where the team actually is; only then can you take it somewhere.

2. Know the Situation

Even though the vision or purpose of an organization may be fairly constant, its situation changes constantly. Good team builders know where the team is and what the situation requires. For example, when a team is young and just getting started, the greatest priority is often to just get good people.

But as a team matures and the level of talent increases, then fine-tuning becomes more important. It's at that time that a leader must spend more time matching the person to the position.

3. KNOW THE PLAYER

It sounds obvious, but you must know the person you are trying to position in the right niche. I mention it because leaders tend to want to make everyone else conform to their image, to approach their work using the same skills and problem-solving methods. But team building is not working on an assembly line.

Mother Teresa, who worked with people her whole life, observed, "I can do what you can't do, and you can do what I can't do; together we can do great things." As you work to build a team, look at each person's experience, skills, temperament, attitude, passion, people skills, discipline, emotional strength, and potential. Only then will you be ready to help a team member to find his or her proper place.

"I CAN DO WHAT YOU CAN'T DO, AND YOU CAN DO WHAT
I CAN'T DO; TOGETHER WE CAN DO GREAT THINGS."
—MOTHER TERESA

Start by Finding the Right Place for You

Right now you may not be in a position to place others on your team. In fact, you may be thinking to yourself, *How do I find my own niche?* If that's the case, then follow these guidelines:

- Be Secure: My friend Wayne Schmidt says, "No amount of personal competency compensates for personal insecurity." If you allow your insecurities to get the better of you, you'll be inflexible and reluctant to change. And you cannot grow with change.

- Get to Know Yourself: You won't be able to find your niche if you don't know your strengths and weaknesses. Spend time reflecting and exploring your gifts. Ask others to give you feedback. Do what it takes to remove personal blind spots.

- Trust Your Leader: A good leader will help you to start moving in the right direction. If you don't trust your leader, look to another mentor for help. Or get on another team.

- See the Big Picture: Your place on the team only makes sense in the context of the big picture. If your only motivation for finding your niche is personal gain, your poor motives may prevent you from discovering what you desire.

- Rely on Your Experience: When it comes down to it, the only way to know that you've discovered your niche is to try what seems right and learn from your failures and successes. When you discover what you were made for, your heart sings. It says, *There's no place like this place anywhere near this place, so this must be the place!*

A Place for Everyone, and Everyone in His Place

One organization that strives to match its people to the right place is the U.S. military. That is particularly true now that it employs an all-volunteer force. If each of the various functions in a military command don't work at top efficiency (and interact well with all the other parts), then terrible breakdowns occur.

When you discover your place you will say, "There's no place like this place anywhere near this place, so this must be the place!"

Nobody is more keenly aware of that than a combat pilot. Take for example Charlie Plumb who retired as a captain of the U.S. Navy. A graduate of Annapolis, he served in Vietnam in the mid-sixties, flying seventy-five missions from the aircraft carrier USS *Kitty Hawk.*

An aircraft carrier is a place where you can readily observe how all the pieces of the military "puzzle" come together to support each other. A carrier is often described as being like a floating city. It contains a crew of 5,500 people, a population greater than that of some of the towns in which its crew members grew up. It must be self-sustaining, and each of its seventeen departments must function as a team accomplishing its mission. And those teams must work together as a team.

Every pilot is acutely aware of the team effort required to put a jet in the air. It takes hundreds of people utilizing dozens of technical specialties to launch, monitor, support, land, and maintain an aircraft. Even more people are involved if that plane is armed for combat. Charlie Plumb was undoubtedly aware that many people worked tirelessly to keep him flying. But despite the efforts of the best-trained air support group in the world, Plumb found himself in a North Vietnamese prison as a POW after his F-4 Phantom jet was shot down on May 19, 1967, during his seventy-fifth mission.

Plumb was held prisoner for nearly six grueling years, part of the time in the infamous Hanoi Hilton. During those years he and his fellow prisoners were humiliated, starved, tortured, and forced to live in squalid conditions. Yet he didn't let the experience break him. He now says, "Our unity through our faith in God and in our love for Country were the great strength which kept us going through some very difficult times."

TURNING POINT

Plumb was released from his imprisonment on February 18, 1973, and continued his career in the navy. But an incident years after his return to the United States marked his life as surely as his imprisonment. One day he and his wife, Cathy, were eating in a restaurant when a man came to the table and said, "You're Plumb. You flew jet fighters in Vietnam."

"That's right," answered Plumb, "I did."

"It was fighter squadron 114 on the *Kitty Hawk*. You were shot down. You were parachuted into enemy hands," the man continued. "You spent six years as a prisoner of war."

The former pilot was taken aback. He looked at the man, trying to identify him, but couldn't. "How in the world did you know that?" Plumb finally asked.

"I packed your parachute."

Plumb was staggered. All he could do was struggle to his feet and shake the man's hand. "I must tell you," Plumb finally said, "I've said a lot of prayers of thanks for your nimble fingers, but I didn't realize I'd have the opportunity of saying thanks in person."[1]

What if the navy had put the wrong person in the position of parachute rigger, the anonymous and the rarely thanked job that man performed during the Vietnam War? Charlie Plumb wouldn't have known about it until it was too late. And we wouldn't even know where the breakdown had occurred, because Plumb wouldn't have lived to tell the tale.

Today, Charlie Plumb is a motivational speaker to Fortune 500 companies, government agencies, and other organizations. He often tells the story of the man who packed his parachute, and he uses it to deliver a message on teamwork. He says, "In a world where downsizing forces us to do more with less, we must empower the team. 'Packing others' parachutes' can mean the difference in survival. Yours and your team's!"[2]

If you desire to pack the parachutes of your people, after you equip them, find the niche where they will flourish. That is the best way to empower them. They will grow to their potential, and your team will go to a whole new level.

Notes

Chapter 2
1. Don Banks, "Teacher First, Seldom Second, Wootten Has Built Monument to Excellence at Maryland's DeMatha High," *St. Petersburg Times*, 3 April 1987, www.dematha.org.
2. John Feinstein, "A Down-to-Earth Coach Brings DeMatha to New Heights," *Washington Post*, 27 February 1984, www.dematha.org.
3. Morgan Wootten and Bill Gilbert, *From Orphans to Champions: The Story of DeMatha's Morgan Wootten* (New York: Atheneum, 1979), 24–25.
4. William Plummer, "Wootten's Way," *People*, 20 November 2000, 166.
5. Wootten and Gilbert, *From Orphans to Champions*, 12–13.

Chapter 4
1. John C. Maxwell, *The Winning Attitude: Your Key to Personal Success* (Nashville, Tennessee: Thomas Nelson, 1993).

Chapter 6
1. "Edwardian Conquest," 14 June 2001, www.britannia.com/wales.

Chapter 7
1. "Packing Parachutes," audiotape excerpt, <www.charlieplumb.com>.
2. "Charlie Plumb's Speech Content," <www.charlieplumb.com>.

John Maxwell's REAL Leadership Series

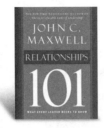

Relationships 101
ISBN 0-7852-6351-9

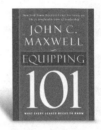

Equipping 101
ISBN 0-7852-6352-7

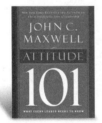

Attitude 101
ISBN 0-7852-6350-0

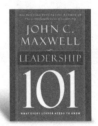

Leadership 101
ISBN 0-7852-6419-1

THOMAS NELSON
PUBLISHERS
Since 1798

Other Books by Dr. John C. Maxwell
Can Teach You How to Be a REAL Success

RELATIONSHIPS
Be a People Person (Victor Books)
Becoming a Person of Influence (Thomas Nelson)
The Power of Partnership in the Church (J. Countryman)
The Treasure of a Friend (J. Countryman)

EQUIPPING
The 17 Indisputable Laws of Teamwork (Thomas Nelson)
The 17 Essential Qualities of a Team Player (Thomas Nelson)
Developing the Leaders Around You (Thomas Nelson)
Partners in Prayer (Thomas Nelson)
Running with the Giants (Warner Books)
Success One Day at a Time (J. Countryman)
There's No Such Thing as Business Ethics (Warner Books)
Thinking for a Change (Warner Books)
Today Matters (Warner Books)

ATTITUDE
Be All You Can Be (Victor Books)
Failing Forward (Thomas Nelson)
The Power of Thinking (Honor Books)
Living at the Next Level (Thomas Nelson)
Think on These Things (Beacon Hill)
The Winning Attitude (Thomas Nelson)
Your Bridge to a Better Future (Thomas Nelson)
The Power of Attitude (Honor Books)

LEADERSHIP
The 21 Indispensable Qualities of a Leader (Thomas Nelson)
The 21 Irrefutable Laws of Leadership (Thomas Nelson)
The 21 Most Powerful Minutes in a Leader's Day (Thomas Nelson)
Developing the Leader Within You (Thomas Nelson)
Leadership Promises for Every Day (J. Countryman)
The Right to Lead (J. Countryman)
Your Road Map for Success (Thomas Nelson)

CONTINUE

We hope you've enjoyed *Equipping 101* and we want you to know that at
INJOY® we believe that equipping leaders for the future is what we're all
about. We are dedicated to developing you as a leader of excellence and
integrity by providing the finest resources and training for your personal
and professional growth.

YOUR

Leadership Wired

Take the next step in developing the leadership potential in yourself and in
those around you. We've made the first step as simple and as easy as possible–
it's FREE and it's delivered to your e-mail box twice a month!
Visit www.Equipping101book.com and sign up for *Leadership Wired* today

LEADERSHIP

Ready for a challenge that's a little meatier? We recommend
Developing the Leaders Around You. Read the valuable lessons
within this book and you'll take the next giant step toward
becoming the leader you've always wanted to be. Order
online today at www.Equipping101book.com.

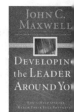

EDUCATION!

SHARE THESE

If you've found valuable insights within the pages
of *Equipping 101,* why not share this treasure with friends, family, and
business associates? Visit us at www.Equipping101book.com and
order a copy for those you value!

LEADERSHIP

Great for holidays, anniversaries, and birthdays, let *Equipping 101* show
those closest to you that you care about their personal and professional
growth. Also, for you sales leaders, remember that *Equipping 101* makes for
a great sales leave behind! Order today at www.Equipping101book.com.

LESSONS

Do you have children preparing to leave home for college,
the military, or the business world? Give them a headstart on
an incredible competitive advantage — equipping leaders for the future!
Visit us at www.Equipping101book.com and order them a copy of
Equipping 101 today.

WITH FRIENDS!

Order *Equipping 101* for a friend
at **www.Equipping101book.com**!

ABOUT THE AUTHOR

John C. Maxwell, known as America's expert on leadership, speaks in person to hundreds of thousands of people each year. He has communicated his leadership principles to Fortune 500 companies, the United States Military Academy at West Point, and sports organizations such as the NCAA, the NBA, and the NFL.

Maxwell is the founder of several organizations, including Maximum Impact, dedicated to helping people reach their leadership potential. He is the author of more than thirty books, including *Developing the Leader Within You*, *Failing Forward*, *Your Road Map for Success*, *There's No Such Thing as Business Ethics*, and *The 21 Irrefutable Laws of Leadership*, which has sold more than one million copies.